Cat Conundrum

Chitra Soundar
Koustubha Jagadeesh

Collins

Contents

Chapter 1 6
Bonus: Radio booth 22
Chapter 2 24
Bonus: Madhu and Marcel's Radio Show 38
Chapter 3 40
Bonus: Burger Bungalow 56
Chapter 4 58
Bonus: Map 72
Chapter 5 74
Bonus: Cat jokes and facts 88
Chapter 6 90
Bonus: Local news 104
About the author 106
About the illustrator 108
Book chat 110

Chapter 1

Still, right now they're our only listeners — four in total: Madhu's dad and grandad, and my parents. One day, soon, not far in the future, we will have double-digit listeners!

Double digits! We'd better get going. We have an amazing segment coming up! Recap on Wednesday's Word of the Day, and introducing Thursday's Thrilling Report, that brings you the news from our neighbourhood. Keep listening!

It was a regular weekday morning at Madhu Pandian and Marcel Tate's radio booth, converted from a red telephone box that Madhu's dad had bought at an auction. It was Madhu's best birthday gift ever. Marcel's dad bid on the radio equipment in the same auction. The two dads loved auctions, antiques and ancient stuff.

It wasn't the Buckingham Palace of booths, to be honest! It was pretty cramped for two people, especially including one with big shoes (size eight already).

Madhu and Marcel didn't mind, though. They loved their little studio that they'd painted bright yellow on the outside with polka dots on the inside.

Well, if you must know, they had to improvise based on the availability of paint, but it wasn't bad for two kids with big ideas. And the rest, as they say, is mystery! Or was that history?

When the two dads showed off their auction finds, SNAP! Madhu and Marcel had the same idea at the same time! A radio show in their own booth! How cool would that be?

A few weeks later, once the paint had dried and the fumes were gone, Madhu and Marcel's Radio Show launched on a lucky day and time picked by Madhu's grandad. From the yellow-polka-dot studio, they broadcast on the internet most mornings, except when they had yoga on Tuesdays and chess class on alternate Wednesdays. They did shows on weekends too, except when they were on holiday. Anyway, back to the show!

First, a recap of yesterday's Word of the Day —

Collywobbles! Who remembers what it means?

I know! I know!

Those who are shouting at their radios, right now, the question was rhetorical. There's no point answering it because we can't hear you!

Let me see, here we go! Paige Turner of Half-Man Lane – I mean Half-Moon Lane, has been fined a thousand pounds for returning a library book six years late.

That's a huge fine! Hope all the page-turning during the six years was worth it. What's next?

Ms Cara Van has reported that her cat Chipmunk has gone missing. She's offering a reward — a small bag of Curlywurlies! Oooh! I love a Curlywurly.

Did you say she lost a chipmunk? Aren't they like squirrels? Did she check if it climbed up a tree??

Ah! It's confusing, isn't it! Actually, Chipmunk is her cat.

Oh, a cat! How did she lose Chipmunk then?

Well, according to my information, the cat disappeared when Ms Van went to work.

Listeners, if you see a cat called Chipmunk, please email us at MAMRadio@radiomail.com.

PING!
Ooh! We've already got an email.
That was fast! Our listeners are the best. What does it say?
It's from our favourite listener!
A favourite listener?? Who is that? What does the email say?
Hang on! Ooops! I pressed the wrong button!
C'mon Marcel. We're losing precious airtime.

"The listener (your grandad) wants to know what sort of cat."

Our little moggie is missing!

Please help us find her!

"Right! If this was a TV show, you would have been able to see that I'm holding up a poster with a picture of a cat. But we are a radio show so we'll describe this to the best of Marcel's abilities. Marcel?"

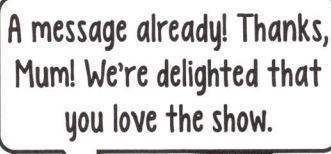

Radio booth

microphone

headphones

sound mixer
A sound mixer records and balances sounds from different sources, like speech, music or special effects. This allows you to control the volume and tone of each source.

laptop with broadcasting software

audio interface
This connects the microphone and audio equipment to the laptop, so sound can be recorded and played.

Chapter 2

After Ms Williams finished taking the register, she set an exercise for the class: write an advertisement to sell or promote something.

Some people wrote about selling their toys, while others wrote about promoting their handmade friendship bands. Madhu and Marcel created an advertisement for their radio show. When they read it out to their class, everyone was impressed. Even their teacher.

"A radio show, how lovely! What did you talk about today on your show?" asked Ms Williams.

They told her about the missing cat called Chipmunk.

"Describe the cat using three adjectives," said Ms Williams, still focused on the English lesson.

"Ginormous grey cat with jaundiced eyes," said Madhu.

"Well done! I like the choice you made to change yellow to jaundiced," said Ms Williams. "So this cat is really missing?"

Marcel nodded solemnly.

"Strange! Because my neighbour's cat is also a humongous grey cat with jaundiced eyes, and it's been missing since lunchtime yesterday!"

But before Madhu and Marcel could find out more, the bell rang, and it was time for break.

During break, Madhu and Marcel went to the library to return their books. The librarian, Mr Taro, waved them over. "Madhu and Marcel, just the two people I wanted to see!"

"I read two books this week already," said Madhu, quickly.

Mr Taro smiled. "Yup, it's not about that. Ms Williams told me about your radio show and the missing cat!"

"News travels fast," said Madhu.

"Have you seen a cat like that?" asked Marcel.

Mr Taro hadn't seen the cats, either of them – Chipmunk, or Ms Williams' neighbour's cat. But he gave them a wonderful tip about the local fire service. The fire service don't only put out fires – sometimes they also rescue animals and people stuck in lifts. "I read about it in a non-fiction book about the fire service! What was your last non-fiction book?"

Mr Taro could turn any conversation around to the topic of books. After listening to a short lecture on how important non-fiction was, the friends quickly checked their books back in and went off to the playground.

That evening, when they were picked up by Marcel's dad, Marcel asked if they could visit the fire station on their way home.

"School project?" asked Marcel's dad.

"Nope! It's for our radio show. We got a tip!"

"A tip of what?"

"A tip of a mystery … dun-dun-dun!" whispered Madhu.

Marcel laughed. "Yes, a thrilling cat mystery … watch this space!"

"A cat mystery set in space, that's so cool!" said Marcel's dad, half listening.

Before Madhu and Marcel could explain, they were pulling in at the fire station. One of the firefighters, with a name tag that said Bob, came out to greet them. "Want a tour?" he asked.

Madhu and Marcel desperately wanted to say yes, but they had more important things to focus on. "We came to ask about your rescues," said Madhu.

"For a school project?" Bob asked.

"Nope! For our radio show!"

"Wow! A radio show! How cool! What sort of rescues are you interested in?"

"Any cats?" asked Marcel.

"Oh, you are asking about Elephantina!" said Bob, showing them a photo of a cat snuggling with the entire crew.

Elephantina was indeed a very large grey cat with yellow eyes!

"Where did you rescue her from?" asked Madhu.

"She was up an electricity pole and was too scared to come down!"

Madhu and Marcel exchanged glances. The cat looked uncannily similar to Chipmunk, Ms Cara Van's cat. Madhu's grandad once said that there may be as many as seven people in the world who looked just like him. Maybe it was the same for cats too.

"Can we meet Elephantina?" asked Marcel.

But Bob said she had gone on a wander. "She comes here for her favourite breakfast – Paw-sta – and then saunters off and comes back whenever she's ready. We are open twenty-four-seven, you see. Sometimes, she doesn't come back until the next day."

"Strange, your cat eats pasta?" said Marcel.

Bob laughed. "Paw-sta is her favourite brand of cat food! Great name, eh?!"

On their way home, Madhu whispered to Marcel, "How is it paw-sible three cats that look exactly the same are missing!"

"Yes, it's a-paw-lling," said Marcel, with a smile!

"Stop the cat puns! They are claw-ful," said Marcel's dad.

Puns aside, they had stumbled upon something very fishy, fur-real.

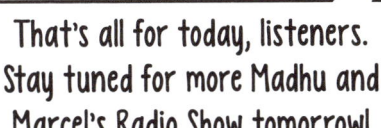

Madhu and Marcel's Radio Show

We are always in the know.

We bring you whimsical world news, jolly jokes and captivating community news.

Check out our weekly schedule:

Wednesday's Word of the Day

Thursday's Thrilling News

Friday Funny

Sensational Saturday Broadcast

Stunning Sunday Segment

Chapter 3

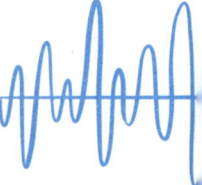

The next morning Madhu and Marcel held a meeting (with their dads). They had a big question on their minds which they needed to discuss before their Sensational Saturday Broadcast. And that question was – how could they be detectives and radio hosts at the same time?

"Maybe you can both investigate and then send me your notes and I can go on air and broadcast it for you?" said Madhu's dad.

"Sorry, Dad," said Madhu. "But it's Madhu and Marcel's Radio Show, we have to be the ones talking."

"Maybe I can investigate," said Madhu's dad.

"Sorry, but we're also the detectives. So we have to do the detecting, investigating, interviewing, gathering clues and finding out what happened!" said Marcel.

"When you say it like that, it sounds like a lot of work," said Madhu. "Are you sure we can do all of this?"

Marcel nodded and extended his hand for a fist bump.

Madhu came in for a handshake and shook his fist.

"Then there's really only one option," said Madhu's dad. "You must take your radio show on the investigation with you."

"How? Do you have a big truck to tow the radio booth with us?" said Madhu.

"You don't need the booth when you're out and about! There's an app for it," said Madhu's dad. "I'll install it on your grandad's phone, and you can broadcast live."

"So we can borrow Grandad's phone?" asked Madhu.

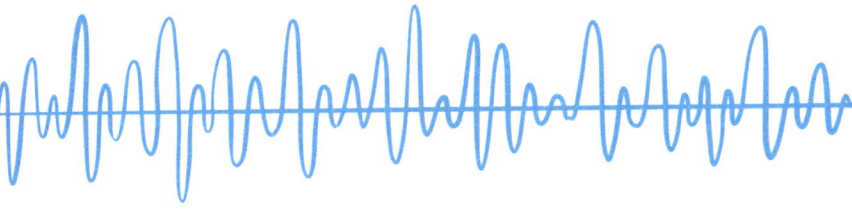

"No, you can borrow Grandad," her dad replied. "And he will bring the phone. You can't go investigating on your own!"

Even though Madhu and Marcel knew that they were children, they were not just any children, they were cat-detective-radio-host children. All the same, they settled for Madhu's dad's solution, that included an app on a phone with a grandad attached to it.

After showing them how to use the app and how to do their show from the phone, Madhu's dad went off to the farmer's market. Madhu and Marcel set off with Grandad and his phone, to gather clues and do some investigating. First stop – Ms Cara Van's residence, which just happened to be a camper van.

We're live from Ms Cara Van's camper van. Here's Marcel asking the questions.

When did you last see Chipmunk?

Right after her lunch of fish chunks I bought at the fishmongers.

How long have you had Chipmunk?

Why does that matter?

Background ... very important.

Ms Van, did you see anyone suspicious around that time?

Around the time I went to the fishmongers? Not really.

Ahem! No, around the time Chipmunk disappeared.

Not really. But I did see a crowd had gathered at the other end of the caravan park, by the wall. A fire engine was blaring its siren. I didn't pay much attention, because I was planting carrots.

Next they went to see Ms Williams' neighbour to ask about Popcorn. Ms Williams introduced them to Popcorn's parents. No, not the actual cat parents, but the human owners.

They had seven other cats – all different sizes, shapes and colours. Madhu wondered how they even noticed that one was missing. Did they take the register like Ms Williams?

"Not very long, actually. She just appeared one day through the cat flap and ate the cat food from all seven bowls."

"A Goldilocks cat!"

"Eh?! Poor Popcorn! She must be starving by now."

Final stop!! Grandad took them to Burger Bungalow for lunch and bought them their favourite – a Bungalow Special burger, carrot chips on the side and a big glass of mango juice.

For a while, no one said anything because they were so busy eating. Once they had eaten, still no one said anything. They were busy slurping their mango juice. At last they were ready to make sense of their enquiries, live on air.

We have our first live listener question! Does Elephantina eat pasta! The answer is —

No! Paw-sta is just a punny name for cat food.

Psst! I have another question! No, actually an observation.

Go on, Grandad!

Strange that a fire engine is involved with all the cats!

"That's the end of today's show, folks! We'll be back tomorrow, live from the fire station!"

"If we can borrow Madhu's grandad and his phone!"

"Signing off, these are your hosts, Madhu and —"

"Marcel!"

Burger Bungalow

Recipe for a Bungalow Special
— serves just one!

Ingredients:

- One tablespoon of olive oil for frying
- Half an onion, finely chopped
- 50 grams of spinach, finely chopped
- One slice of mango, chopped into tiny pieces
- One slice of white bread blitzed into breadcrumbs (or 15 grams of dried breadcrumbs)
- Ten grams of mature cheddar
- Half a large egg, beaten
- One tablespoon of plain flour

To serve:

- Tomatoes – sliced
- Lettuce leaves
- Slices of your favourite cheese

Steps:

1. Gently fry the onions until they are soft. Then add them to a bowl.
2. Add finely chopped spinach, breadcrumbs, cheddar, mango pieces and mash together.
3. Add the beaten egg and mix until combined.
4. Roll into a ball and flatten into a burger.
5. Coat the burger in flour.
6. Then heat some oil on a pan and fry the burger on both sides until both sides are brown.

The burger is ready to serve between two slices of your favourite bun, topped with your favourite cheese slices, tomato slices and lettuce leaves.

Enjoy The Bungalow Special burger!

 # Chapter 4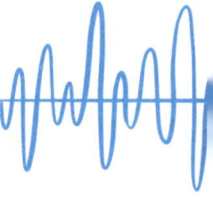

That Sunday morning, Madhu woke up early and went to wake Grandad, who was fast asleep with a book over his face.

"Grandad, wake up!" called Madhu.

Grandad sat up, confused. "Where is the fire?"

"There's no fire here! But we are due at the fire station! Remember, for the investigation?"

Grandad groaned. "It's eight a.m. on a Sunday morning!"

"C'mon, Grandad, it's an important investigation!"

As Madhu came into the living room, Marcel walked in.

"Ready to go?" he asked.

"Just waiting for our live radio equipment!" said Madhu.

"Coming!" said Grandad, from inside.

Soon they were on their way to the fire station, hoping that the entire town was still in bed and there had been no emergencies.

"Are you two going to interview the fire crew?" asked Grandad.

"That's the plan," said Madhu.

"But if one of them is the kitty-napper, will they reveal that to you? Especially if you're detectives?" asked Grandad.

"Hmm, Bob did act strangely yesterday," said Marcel. "He was listening to find out what we had learnt about the cats, and then as soon as we talked about the firefighters, he disappeared."

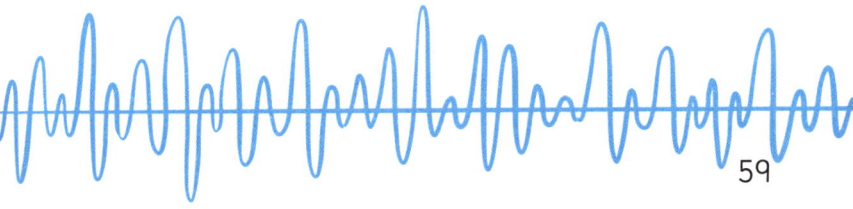

"Right, then we won't tell them we are doing it for the investigation," said Madhu.

"But Bob will know," said Marcel, as they turned the corner into the street where the fire station was located.

The fire station was busy. Firefighters were bustling about.

"Hello Bob!" called Marcel.

A firefighter peeped from behind the fire engine. "Can I help you?"

"Is she Bob?" whispered Grandad.

"She isn't," said Madhu. She turned to the firefighter and said, "We're Madhu and Marcel from the Madhu and Marcel's Radio Show!"

The firefighter shrugged. "Never heard of it," she said.

"Bob has! Bob is a listener!"

"Bob's not in today! He's training for a cycling race," said the woman. "How can I help you both?"

Madhu and Marcel exchanged glances and huddled for a quick chat.

"Isn't it suspicious that Bob isn't here?" asked Marcel.

"There's nothing suspicious about training for a cycling race," said Grandad. "In my day, I used to train every day for hours."

"Bob's not here, so let's talk to the others first. If Bob is the kitty-napper, maybe he has an accomplice," said Madhu.

"Yup! Good plan," Marcel whispered and turned back to the firefighter. "We wanted to interview everyone!"

"For our school project," Madhu finished.

"Right, if Bob agreed, we can't turn you away now! We love to engage with our local community, particularly children," said the firefighter.
"My name is Ember!"

"Wow! A cool fiery name!" said Grandad.

"I get that a lot," said Ember. "Would you like a tour?"

And this time Madhu and Marcel couldn't resist. Ember showed them the bays for the fire engine, the storage for all the equipment, showers, toilets. There was a meeting room with a long rectangular table in the middle and lots of chairs around it. This room had a map on the wall, with pins stuck into it.

"What does that map show?" asked Marcel.

"It's all the places we have responded to an emergency this month!"

"Can I take a picture?" Grandad asked, getting his phone ready.

"Go ahead – if it's a good one, we'll post it on our social media."

Madhu and Marcel were looking at some old photos of the fire station on the wall.

"This fire station was opened in 1836," said Ember. "Legend goes, a cat called Signal once warned the firemen of a fire that broke out inside the station."

"Wow! A cat saved nine lives," said Marcel.

After the tour was over, Madhu and Marcel gathered in the meeting room with the entire fire crew: Flint, Mishal, Ember, Reese and Brenna. Bob wasn't in, they knew already.

There's no such thing as a Dalmatian cat!
Yes, there is, Ember!

No, you can't make up breeds!

Firefighter Flint and Firefighter Mishal, what about you?

No idea! I'm not into animals.

You might not love animals, but you do like fluffy and furry hats that we sometimes mistake for a cat when you leave them on a chair!

And that was the end of the interview.
An alarm went off somewhere and the fire crew quickly left the room to attend to the call.

Madhu and Marcel walked back home with Grandad, pondering over the information they had gathered so far.

"What's your next step?" asked Grandad.

"We need to think about everything we have learnt!" said Madhu.

"Back to the studio!" said Marcel.

"Right after lunch!" said Grandad. "I'm starving."

It turned out that the two dads had arranged a picnic lunch in the garden for everyone, except Marcel's mum, who was working.

"Time to recharge our batteries," said Madhu, filling her plate with a bit of everything.

"Are you going to tell us about what you investigated today?" asked Marcel's dad, biting into his sandwich.

"Nope! You have to listen to our radio show this afternoon!" said Marcel.

Chapter 5

"So let's say a cat had four to five kittens, and they all went to different homes. And now —"

"The mother cat is stealing them back! Our kitty-knapper is another cat?"

"Wow! You've broken the case wide open! When we solve this case, we'll be the first ones who have caught a mother cat kitty-napper."

Madhu and Marcel couldn't contain their excitement. They were so close to solving the mystery of the missing cats. A mother cat stealing back her kittens! This was the stuff of movies! But their excitement didn't last long, because Madhu's dad stood by the garage door with a serious face.

"What's wrong, Dad?" asked Madhu.

Marcel's dad arrived with the two posters he had seen during his park run. "Madhu, Marcel, these missing cats are uncannily similar!" he said.

"Yes, because they are siblings! From one mum," said Marcel. "Weren't you listening? Were you on your phone all the time?"

"Hmm, is it even possible for a mother cat to kidnap so many other large cats?" asked Madhu's dad.

"You mean kitty-nap," said Marcel.

"And why would she do it now, after all this time?" asked Marcel's dad.

"Good question! To be proper detectives we need to figure out: Motive, Means and Opportunity," said Madhu.

The investigating radio-show hosts and their dads moved to the living room, where Marcel's mum and Madhu's grandad had set up some snacks.

"You can always think better when you're not hungry," said Grandad.

"Thanks, Grandad!" called Madhu and Marcel.

Madhu's dad asked them to consider some human suspects too. Who had a motive? Who had the means and who had the opportunity?

"Right, so our hunch is that it's the mother cat, but let's see if any of the humans could have done it," said Marcel.

"The firefighters are good candidates," piped in Marcel's mum. "Based on the interviews!"

"Yeah! Furry Hat Flint – could that hat possibly be real fur?!" asked Marcel.

"Cat in a Hat has a whole new meaning now," said Madhu.

Marcel shuddered. "No, that can't be true, can it?!"

"Truth is stranger than fiction," said Grandad. "Anything is possible!"

"Then there's Bob," said Madhu. "He's acting suspiciously. Maybe he's the one taking the cats while he's on duty? He does love cats, and the fire engines were spotted each time a cat went missing."

"So does Reese, with the Dalmatian cat!" said Marcel's mum.

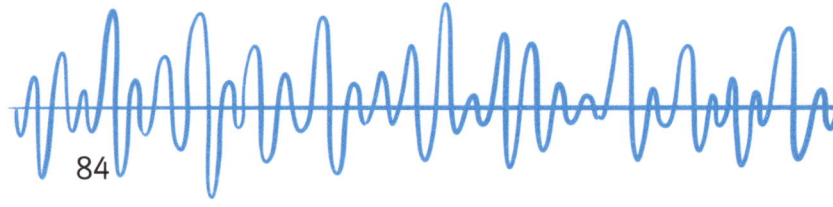

"That means we can't yet rule out anyone!" said Madhu.

"I looked it up, there's no such thing as a Dalmatian cat," said Marcel. "They are called cow cats!"

"Cow cats? Will they mew or moo?" asked Madhu's dad.

"Very funny, Dad!" said Madhu. "But if Reese doesn't know one type of cat from another, how did she target these specific cats?"

Marcel gasped!

"What?" everyone chorused.

"I forgot ketchup!" said Marcel.

Everyone groaned in disappointment.

Madhu gasped.

"What, ketchup again?" asked Marcel's mum.

Madhu shook her head. "No! I think it could be someone who wants to sell British shorthair cats to foreign dealers or zoos!"

"I didn't realise there was a demand for these cats," said Grandad.

"Or that zoos kept cats," said Marcel's mum.

"But what about our mother cat kitty-napper theory? We were going to be famous?" wailed Marcel. "I get up for a bottle of ketchup and you've completely changed the theory!"

"Don't you think a human culprit is more plausible?" asked Madhu.

"I think anything is paw-sible for a mother cat!" said Marcel.

"Right, our suspect is either a human or a cat," said Madhu. "Either way, they like fire engines. So, why don't we plan a stake-out?!"

"A steak-out?" cried Madhu's dad. "I'm vegan!"

"Not that kind of steak, Dad, we want to lie low and watch the fire station! Maybe we can locate either the prowling mother cat or the firefighter who is kitty-napping."

"Yes, let's do it tomorrow," said Marcel. "It's the bank holiday weekend anyway and we don't have to go to school."

Grandad sighed. "Fine! I'll set an early alarm for tomorrow. When this is finished, I warn you, I'm going to have a lie-in every day."

"Thank you, Grandad," said Madhu, giving him a hug.

BONUS
Cat jokes

How do you sort cats?
By cat-egories.

Why was the new cat copying the dog?
Because it was a copycat.

How do cats make others do what they want?
They are very purr-suasive.

What concerts do cats go to?
Mewsic concerts, of course!

Which cat becomes the leader in a pack?
The cat with the biggest purr-sonality.

Cat facts!

Did you know?

Cats are red-green colour-blind.

They can rotate their ears 180 degrees to pinpoint sounds.

Cats can jump five times their height.

And they have an amazing sense of balance!

 # Chapter 6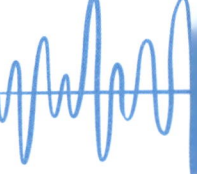

Next morning, Grandad, Madhu and Marcel set out super-early on their bikes.

They found a spot not far from the fire station where they could keep an eye on the comings and goings. One by one, all of the fire crew arrived for work. Except Bob!

Bob arrived late, on his bike, with a yellow pannier on each side. He parked the bike and something sprang out of the pannier and scampered inside.

"Did you see that?" asked Marcel.

"Yes, one grey cat, but where are the others?" asked Madhu.

It was obvious that Bob was connected to this mystery. But how?

An alarm interrupted their thoughts. The fire crew had been summoned.

"On your bikes! Be prepared to tail the fire engine!" said Madhu.

"But can we keep up?"

"Of course we can! The traffic will slow them down," said Grandad.

The firefighters jumped on board the fire engine and the driver pulled out into the road. Just then, there was a sudden flash of grey – the cat had jumped onto the fire engine.

"Wow!" said Marcel.

"Ready to go, Grandad? We'll lose them otherwise," said Madhu, not noticing the cat.

"Nope! I think I know where they're going," said Grandad. "They're off to Malkin Street."

"How do you know that?"

"It's the only logical destination from this direction," said Grandad, holding up his phone like a trophy. "Right, let's take the shortcut."

They followed the fire engine's siren as they turned towards Malkin Street, on the other side of the caravan park. When the fire engine parked, the grey cat jumped out of its hiding spot, jumped over a low wall and disappeared.

"Hurry! Follow that cat," said Madhu.

They cycled down the street just in time to see the cat entering Ms Cara Van's camper van.

"What's happening?" said Marcel.

"Is this the mother cat, do you think?" asked Madhu.

They waited, watching the door. Suddenly, the fire engine's siren blared, startling them. The cat darted out and jumped up again onto the fire engine for a ride back to the fire station.

"Go, go, go!" yelled Marcel, as they hurried behind the engine again.

Madhu, Marcel and Grandad returned to the fire station to keep watch. They sat under the shade of a plane tree waiting either for the cat to leave the fire station or the fire engine to be called out again.

Unfortunately – for them – it was all quiet that bank holiday Monday afternoon.

"I'm bored," said Madhu.

"We can't leave the stakeout now," said Marcel. "We've got to figure this out."

So they waited. But they were even more bored, counting red cars, making up shapes in the clouds and blowing the seeds of dandelions growing on the pavement.

"It's almost teatime," said Marcel.

"Let's give it another 20 minutes," said Grandad.

"Then let's do a broadcast," suggested Madhu.

The fire engine was leaving again, and once more, the grey cat jumped onboard.

"They are headed to Ocelot Lane," said Grandad.

Amazingly, Ocelot Lane was not far from Popcorn's house. The cat did exactly the same thing – it got off the fire engine unnoticed, scuttled across a street, squirmed through a gap in the hedge and entered Popcorn's house.

"I can't believe ELEPHANTINA is so cunning! She somehow has found out about the missing cats, and is impersonating them!" said Marcel.

"That means we have two naughty cats: a mother cat looking for her grown-up kittens, and a cunning, impersonating cat, that's eating food in all the houses!"

Grandad coughed to get their attention.

"Actually – "

But Madhu and Marcel couldn't contain themselves. "This is huge news! We must broadcast right away!"

"Can we go home and do that?" asked Grandad. "I really need to use the loo!"

PING!
PING!
PING!
What's happening?

Emails are coming in. All the missing cats have a black patch on their bellies.
What does that mean?
Listeners! Let's consider this!

Local News

Radio-Show Hosts Solve a Cat Mystery!

Madhu Pandian and Marcel Tate have solved the mystery of a missing cat – or cats! The two children broadcast their own radio show focusing on local news. One day they came up with a major scoop – not one but five grey cats seemed to be missing from the neighbourhood! Madhu and Marcel quickly decided to investigate.

Interviewing the owners of the cats revealed that the local fire station was connected to them. The two radio hosts interviewed the brave firefighters.

Madhu Pandian said , "This case stumped us! Were the cats the victims of a serial kitty-napper or a mummy cat trying to find her kittens that had been taken away from her a while ago, or worse?"

Their stakeouts have uncovered something much more cat-like! One of the cats, Elephantina, had been taking a ride on the fire engine to munch on her favourite foods at different homes. She had adopted families who would give her a variety of meals, even though she did technically have a home!

"Clever kitty! Although I do like the idea of The Revenge of the Mummy Cat," said Marcel, with a smile.

All's well that ends with a meal! Don't forget to tune into Madhu and Marcel's Radio Show for your local news and mysteries.

About the author

What made you want to be an author?

From six years old, I loved books and telling stories. I grew up in a family of storytellers and that inspired me to make up my own stories. So I decided to become an author.

What's your favourite thing about writing?

Chitra Soundar

I love making up new characters and finding out who they are, how they speak and what they are up to. I love creating worlds in which I'd like to live and be friends with my characters.

How did you come up for the idea for this book?

I started with the idea of two friends having a radio show and covering local news. From there my love for mysteries and funny wordplay took over and the book idea sprang to life.

Are any characters based on people you know?

All characters are a little bit borrowed from real life. They might not be people I know, though. I observe people on trains and buses, and meet people on my visits to schools. Every character has a little bit of me too. Marcel loves wordplay like me and Madhu focuses on her mission, also like me.

Does anything in the book relate to your own experiences?
Sadly, my life is not as interesting as my stories are. I'm kidding! I love the idea of a radio show – because I love talking about any topic. I would love to have a best friend with whom I could do a show. I used to live near a fire station, and that's as far as it goes for connections. Most of this story is made up.

Would you like to host a radio show? What would it be like?
I'd love to host a radio show. I would discuss stories from around the world and play world music.

What do you hope readers will get from the book?
I really hope children who are reading this book will create a radio show of their own! They can also visit radio stations near them, if possible, to find out more. And definitely I hope readers are interested in their local community and read the local newspapers.

If you could write another Madhu and Marcel story, what would it be about?
Ooh! If there is another Madhu and Marcel Radio Show story, perhaps the mystery would be about finding who stole the golden toilet from a local museum.

About the illustrator

Did you always want to be an illustrator?
Yes, I always wanted to be an artist of some kind. It was only after studying engineering and working in an office for a while that I moved back into doing art.

How did you get into illustrating?
I bought a tablet while I was working as an engineer and taught myself how to paint digitally. It took years of practice before I realised that I wanted to be a children's book illustrator.

Koustubha Jagadeesh

Do you use pens and paints or do you work digitally?
I primarily paint digitally, and worked digitally for this book as well.

What was the most challenging thing about illustrating this book?
Painting the telephone booth radio station and thinking about the layout and how it would function was challenging.

What was your favourite scene to illustrate?
I thoroughly enjoyed illustrating the scene of the picnic lunch in the garden.

Do you do lots of research when you are illustrating?
If I enjoy anything other than illustrating in the whole book creation process, it has to be the research. I do extensive research on all necessary topics to make my illustrations as good as they can be.

Which character in the book did you identify with the most?
I think it has to be Marcel – he believes in himself and is ready to take up a challenge.

Which character was the most fun to draw?
I loved creating Madhu's grandad. He is such an adorable and fun grandparent to have.

Do the characters you draw look like people you know in real life?
Fun fact here … After drawing all the firefighters, I kept thinking that one of the firefighters looks a bit like someone I know. Later it came to me that Brenna looks a bit like the author – Chitra Soundar! Chitra must have been on my mind while I was working on the book. People I know or see usually make their way into the characters in my illustrations.

Book chat

What did you enjoy most about this book?

Would you like to host a radio show?

Did you have a favourite character? If so, who and why?

What theories did you have about the cat mystery as you read?

Do you have a favourite picture in the book?

If you could speak to the author, what would you ask?

Who would you recommend this book to and why?

How would you summarise this book in three words?

Book challenge:
Imagine you host a radio show with a friend. Design a poster to advertise it.

Published by Collins
An imprint of HarperCollins*Publishers*

The News Building
1 London Bridge Street
London
SE1 9GF
UK

Macken House
39/40 Mayor Street Upper
Dublin 1
D01 C9W8
Ireland

© HarperCollins*Publishers* Limited 2025

10 9 8 7 6 5 4 3 2 1

ISBN 978-0-00-876781-5

All rights reserved. No part of this publication may be reproduced, stored in a retrieval system, or transmitted in any form by any means, electronic, mechanical, photocopying, recording or otherwise, without the prior written permission of the Publisher or a licence permitting restricted copying in the United Kingdom issued by the Copyright Licensing Agency Ltd, 5th Floor, Shackleton House, 4 Battle Bridge Lane, London SE1 2HX.

Without limiting the exclusive rights of any author, contributor or the publisher of this publication, any unauthorised use of this publication to train generative artificial intelligence (AI) technologies is expressly prohibited. HarperCollins also exercise their rights under Article 4(3) of the Digital Single Market Directive 2019/790 and expressly reserve this publication from the text and data mining exception.

British Library Cataloguing-in-Publication Data
A catalogue record for this publication is available from the British Library.

Download the teaching notes and word cards to accompany this book at:
http://littlewandle.org.uk/signupfluency/

Get the latest Collins Big Cat news at
collins.co.uk/collinsbigcat

Author: Chitra Soundar
Illustrator: Koustubha Jagadeesh (Illo Agency)
Publisher: Laura White
Commissioning editor and
    product manager: Caroline Green
Series editor: Charlotte Raby
Development editor: Catherine Baker
Project manager: Emily Hooton
Copyeditor: Sally Byford
Proofreader: Catherine Dakin
Reviewer: Martin Stebbings
Cover and internal designer: Sarah Finan
Production controller: Katharine Willard

Printed in the UK.

MIX
Paper | Supporting responsible forestry
FSC™ C007454

This book contains FSC™ certified paper and other controlled sources to ensure responsible forest management.

For more information visit: www.harpercollins.co.uk/green

Made with responsibly sourced paper and vegetable ink

Scan to see how we are reducing our environmental impact.